REMARKABLE PEOPLE

Leonardo DiCaprio

by Faith Woodland

AV² provides enriched content that supplements and complements this book. Weigl's AV² books strive to create inspired learning and engage young minds in a total learning experience.

Your AV² Media Enhanced books come alive with...

Audio
Listen to sections of the book read aloud.

Key Words
Study vocabulary, and complete a matching word activity.

Video
Watch informative video clips.

Quizzes
Test your knowledge.

Embedded Weblinks
Gain additional information for research.

Slide Show
View images and captions, and prepare a presentation.

Try This!
Complete activities and hands-on experiments.

... and much, much more!

Go to **www.av2books.com,** and enter this book's unique code.

BOOK CODE

X909005

AV² by Weigl brings you media enhanced books that support active learning.

Published by AV² by Weigl
350 5th Avenue, 59th Floor
New York, NY 10118

www.av2books.com   www.weigl.com

Library of Congress Cataloging-in-Publication Data

Woodland, Faith.
 Leonardo DiCaprio / Faith Woodland.
    pages cm. -- (Remarkable people)
 Summary: "Explores the life and times of Leonardo DiCaprio, providing an in-depth look at the inspiration, achievements, and successes that define him. Intended for fourth to sixth grade students"-- Provided by publisher.
 Includes index.
 ISBN 978-1-62127-390-5 (hardcover : alk. paper) -- ISBN 978-1-62127-396-7 (softcover : alk. paper)
 1. DiCaprio, Leonardo--Juvenile literature. 2. Motion picture actors and actresses--United States--Biography--Juvenile literature. I. Title.
 PN2287.D4635W66 2013
 791.4302'8092--dc23
 [B]
                                        2012041040

Printed in the United States of America in North Mankato, Minnesota
1 2 3 4 5 6 7 8 9 0 17 16 15 14 13

032013
WEP300113

Editor: Heather Kissock
Design: Terry Paulhus

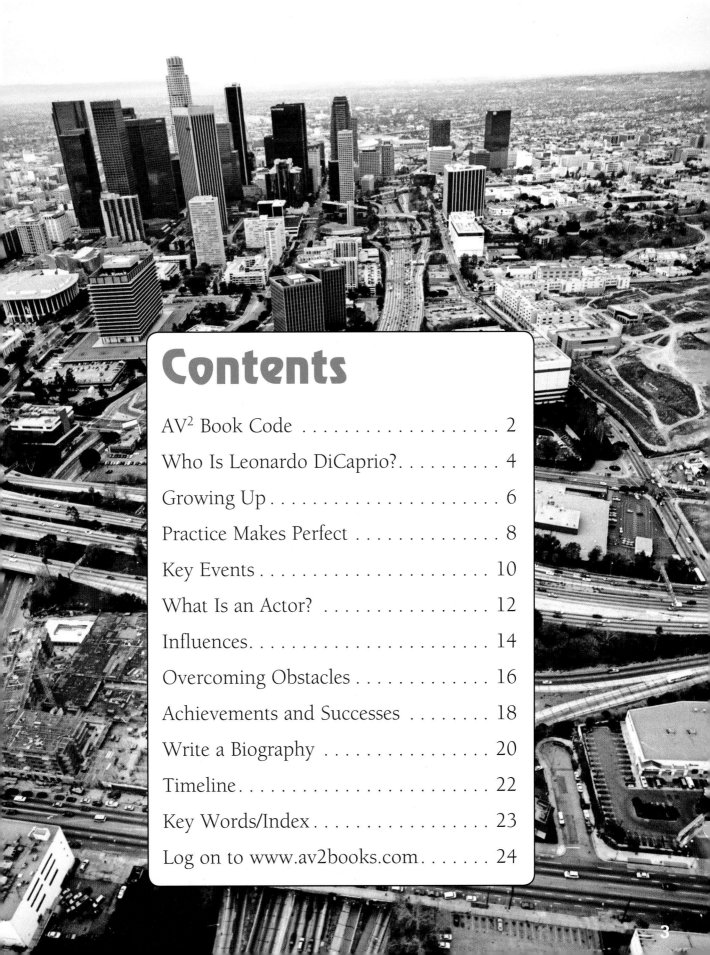

Contents

Who Is Leonardo DiCaprio?

Leonardo DiCaprio is one of the world's best-known actors. He is in constant demand to play **roles** in major motion pictures. **Movie directors** like the way he takes risks in his acting. He is known for choosing roles that are difficult to play.

"I like to be abl[e] play a characte[r] and act out a lo[t of] things which I c[an't] do in my norma[l] everyday life."

With a career spanning more than 30 years, Leonardo has had starring roles in many **blockbusters**. He is most often recognized for playing Jack Dawson in the film *Titanic*. Released in 1997, the movie won 11 **Academy Awards**, including Best Picture.

Besides being an actor, Leonardo is also an **environmental activist**. In 1998, he and his family established their own environmental group called The Leonardo DiCaprio Foundation. This organization focuses attention on animals in danger, clean water, and **renewable energy**.

Growing Up

Leonardo Wilhelm DiCaprio was born on November 11, 1974, in Los Angeles, California. He is the only child of Irmelin and George DiCaprio. Irmelin worked as a legal secretary, and George was a comic book artist. Months before Leonardo's birth, his parents visited a museum in Italy. While looking at a painting by the artist Leonardo da Vinci, Irmelin felt her baby kick. She decided to name her baby after the artist.

When Leonardo was still a baby, his parents divorced. Leonardo remained close with both parents, but he was raised mainly by his mother. They lived in several neighborhoods in the Los Angeles area.

As a child, Leonardo was always clowning around and **imitating** people. His parents enjoyed watching Leonardo entertain people. They supported him when he wanted to try acting and helped him find an **agent**. It was not long before Leonardo was appearing in commercials and playing small parts in movies and television shows.

■ Leonardo's mother has always encouraged his acting career. She often accompanies him to movie openings and awards shows.

Get to Know California

FLOWER
California
Poppy

TREE
California
Redwood

BIRD
California
Quail

Sacramento is the capital city of California. It became the capital in 1854.

California has more than 1,200 miles (1,931 kilometers) of coastline.

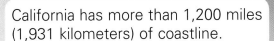

California has the highest and lowest points in the continental United States. Mount Whitney rises 14,494 feet (4,418 meters) above sea level, while Death Valley is 282 feet (86 m) below sea level.

With about 3.8 million residents, Los Angeles is California's largest city, and the second largest city in the United States.

Think about it!

Los Angeles is the movie capital of the United States. Many people move to Los Angeles to try a career in show business. How do you think living in Los Angeles affected Leonardo when he was growing up? Did living in Los Angeles influence his decision to become an actor? What is your hometown known for? How has it influenced the choices you have made in your life?

Practice Makes Perfect

In 1991, Leonardo caught his first real break in show business. He was **cast** as Luke Brower on a television **sitcom** called *Growing Pains*. The show had been airing since 1985 and had an established audience. People were now seeing Leonardo on TV every week. He started to gain a fan following.

He also began to attract attention from movie directors. Only a year after appearing on *Growing Pains*, Leonardo was cast in a movie called *This Boy's Life*. It starred acting legend Robert De Niro. In 1993, Leonardo starred with Johnny Depp in *What's Eating Gilbert Grape*. The movie met with modest success and made more than $9 million in sales.

■ Leonardo was nominated for six awards for his role in *What's Eating Gilbert Grape*, and won a Chicago Film Critics Association Award for Most Promising Actor.

Leonardo's first major starring role came in 1996, when he appeared in *William Shakespeare's Romeo + Juliet*. Directed by Baz Luhrmann, the movie brought Shakespeare's play into a modern setting. Leonardo played Romeo, and Claire Danes played Juliet. The movie made more than $145 million worldwide and launched Leonardo as a true movie star.

■ Leonardo was Baz Luhrmann's first choice to play Romeo. He was cast because of his rebellious look and strong acting skills.

Key Events

When director James Cameron first offered Leonardo the male lead in his movie *Titanic*, Leonardo hesitated. *Titanic* was not the kind of movie Leonardo wanted to be in. He did not want to be part of a big Hollywood production. Over time, however, James was able to change Leonardo's mind. Leonardo was cast as Jack Dawson, a young man who wins a free ride on the doomed ship.

Titanic became a major success. It made more than $1.8 billion worldwide. This was more than any other movie had made in history. Leonardo was now an international superstar. He was especially admired by female fans. "Leo-Mania" broke out, and teenagers lined up anywhere Leonardo went to get a glimpse of, or an autograph from, their favorite star.

Over the next few years, Leonardo made several other movies. However, none reached the level of success that *Titanic* had. This did not bother Leonardo. He was focused on finding roles that let him test his acting skills.

■ While filming *Titanic*, Leonardo became close friends with actress Kate Winslet. They remain close to this day.

Thoughts from Leonardo

Leonardo has said many things about acting, being a celebrity, and his desire to help the environment. Here are some examples.

Leonardo knows who he is.

"I'm not the sort of person who tries to be cool or trendy, I'm definitely an individual."

Leonardo talks about the benefits of being an actor.

"The best thing about acting is that I get to lose myself in another character, and actually get paid for it."

Leonardo talks about the importance of friends and family.

"What keeps me grounded is my friends and family and being able to joke around and have a sense of humor. ...Being able to have the sanctity of people you know and love and trust really makes you feel safe in your environment."

Leonardo knows how to separate himself from the parts he plays.

"Don't think for a moment that I'm really like any of the characters I play. I'm not. That's why it's called 'acting'."

Leonardo discusses being a celebrity.

"Everywhere I go, somebody is staring at me. I don't know if people are staring because they recognize me, or because they think I'm a weirdo."

Leonardo is committed to the environment.

"Raising awareness on the most pressing environmental issues of our time is more important than ever."

What Is an Actor?

An actor is someone who portrays a character in a story. Actors play characters in roles on TV, in movies, and in plays. Often, actors must learn lines and movements that are written in **scripts**. Sometimes, actors do not use a script. They say and do what they feel in the moment. This is called improvisation.

Acting requires certain skills and training. It is necessary to memorize lines and cues, so the actors know when to speak, move, or enter a scene. They must learn to move carefully so as not to block other actors from the camera or audience. Most importantly, an actor must become skilled at creating a character. Some actors attend special classes for their training. Others take private acting lessons.

For most actors, success does not come quickly or easily. Actors must keep trying. An actor may **audition** for many roles before he or she is hired.

■ Movie actors work closely with their directors to bring a story to life. In 2011, Leonardo worked with director Clint Eastwood on the movie *J. Edgar*, about the first head of the Federal Bureau of Investigation (FBI).

Actors 101

Kate Winslet (1975–)

Born into a family of stage actors, Kate Winslet began acting in childhood. Her first television experience was in a cereal commercial. Kate studied acting at a performing arts high school. She was working in movies before she graduated. In 1995, she had a starring role in *Sense and Sensibility* and received her first Academy Award **nomination**. Two years later, she was cast beside Leonardo in *Titanic*. She received her second Academy Award nomination for her portrayal of Rose. In 2009, she won her first Academy Award for her role in *The Reader*. Like Leonardo, Kate continues to seek roles that challenge her as an actor.

Tobey Maguire (1975–)

Tobey Maguire was born in Santa Monica, California. He began acting when he was a teenager. He often competed for roles with Leonardo, and the two became good friends. Tobey's movie career took off when he played the title role in the first three *Spiderman* movies. The success of these movies led to other parts in major motion pictures. Tobey appeared in blockbuster movies such as *Seabiscuit* and *The Great Gatsby*.

Claire Danes (1979–)

Claire Danes was born and raised in New York. She had an early interest in acting and studied at a performing arts school in the city. In 1992, she was cast as the lead in a television show called *My So-Called Life*. Even though the show only lasted one year, it launched Claire's career. In 1996, she played the female lead in Baz Luhrmann's *William Shakespeare's Romeo + Juliet*, opposite Leonardo. Since then, she has gone on to appear in numerous movies, including the 2010 release *Temple Grandin*. Her work in this TV movie won her an Emmy, **Golden Globe**, and Screen Actors Guild Award. Since 2011, she has been the star of the television series *Homeland*.

Josh Hutcherson (1992–)

Josh Hutcherson was born in Kentucky. He knew he wanted to act since he was four years old. When he was nine years old, his family moved to Los Angeles to help him find acting jobs. His first jobs were small parts in television shows and movies. His breakthrough role came in 2007 when he was cast as the male lead in *Bridge to Terabithia*. In 2012, Josh won the role of Peeta Mellark in *The Hunger Games*. The movie made more than $685 million worldwide.

Moviemaking

Writers, directors, producers, crewmembers, actors, and editors work hard to make movies. They can take months, or even years, to create. Movies have been made in the United States since the early 1900s. The first movies were called silent films because they did not have sound.

Influences

Leonardo's family encouraged his **creativity** from an early age. When Irmelin and George realized their son had an interest in acting, they were supportive and helped him get started. This support continued even when the couple divorced. When George remarried, Leonardo gained a stepbrother named Adam Farrar who was already acting in television. Adam also encouraged Leonardo's interest in acting.

Robert De Niro and Jack Nicholson are two of the actors that Leonardo admires the most. He likes the fact that they take risks with their acting and want to do their best to portray their characters accurately. Leonardo has worked on movies with both of these men. He acted with Robert in *This Boy's Life* and *Marvin's Room*. Jack was his co-star in *The Departed*.

■ At the 2010 Golden Globes, Leonardo and Robert presented Martin with the Cecil B. DeMille Award for his outstanding contribution to the world of entertainment.

From a young age, Leonardo's goal was to work with movie director Martin Scorsese. Martin is known for making dramatic movies. Leonardo wanted the challenge of having to deliver intense and raw emotions. He was honored when Martin began casting him in movies such as *Gangs of New York* and *The Departed*.

MEET THE DICAPRIO FAMILY

Leonardo has remained close to his parents. He credits his mother with keeping him grounded in the fast-moving show business world. He has said that his creativity comes from his father. Being an artist himself, George would often invite other artists to his home. This exposed Leonardo to people who thought differently about life and took risks.

■ Leonardo credits his father with teaching him how to be patient and tolerant of other people's views.

Overcoming Obstacles

When Leonardo first began his acting career, an agent suggested that he change his name to Lenny Williams. The agent felt that Leonardo's real name sounded too foreign. He said that Lenny Williams sounded more American and would help Leonardo get acting jobs. The agent told Leonardo that he would not get many jobs with his real name.

Leonardo and his family refused to change his name. Instead, they found Leonardo another agent to help him find acting jobs. When people in the movie industry realized his talent, his name helped them remember him. Today, his unique name has helped him become recognized worldwide.

■ Leonardo's acting talents have given him the opportunity to work with some of Hollywood's biggest names. In 2002, he teamed up with famed director Steven Spielberg for the film *Catch Me If You Can*.

Leonardo is constantly in demand as an actor. This is because he commits himself fully to his job. Sometimes, however, his busy acting schedule leads to exhaustion. In 2013, Leonardo announced that he was going to take a long break from acting. He wanted to relax and explore other interests for a while. He also wanted to devote more time to helping the environment.

■ Despite taking a break from the silver screen, Leonardo remains dedicated to his fans. In 2013, he went to Seoul, South Korea to promote his film *Django Unchained*.

Achievements and Successes

Over the course of his acting career, Leonardo DiCaprio has been nominated for many national and international awards. In 1994, he received his first of three Academy Award nominations, for playing Arnie in *What's Eating Gilbert Grape*. His leading role in *William Shakespeare's Romeo + Juliet* earned him the Best Actor Award at the Berlin International Film Festival three years later.

In 2004, Leonardo starred as billionaire Howard Hughes in Martin Scorsese's *The Aviator*. This role gave him his first Golden Globe Award. Two years later, he was nominated again for the same award. He received two Golden Globe nominations in the same category for his roles in *The Departed* and *Blood Diamond*.

■ Leonardo's role in *The Aviator* earned him 13 award nominations around the world. In addition to the Golden Globe, he won an MTV Movie Award for Best Male Performance.

Leonardo has been called one of the top actors of his generation. He is also one of Hollywood's best paid. In fact, in 2011, Leonardo was ranked as the highest earning actor in Hollywood. He was reported to have made about $77 million in 2010.

HELPING OTHERS

Leonardo DiCaprio has made an effort to help people who have experienced hardship. After an earthquake destroyed a public library in Los Angeles in 1994, Leonardo donated money to the library to fund a new computer center. Following the 2010 earthquake in Haiti, he donated $1 million to **relief** efforts. Later that year, he donated another $1 million to the Wildlife Conservation Society to help save **endangered animals**.

Through the efforts of The Leonardo DiCaprio Foundation, Leonardo works to bring attention to environmental issues. The foundation is dedicated to helping people, animals, and the planet. Environmental groups have praised Leonardo for his activism. In 2010, he was awarded the VH1 Do Something Award.

Write a Biography

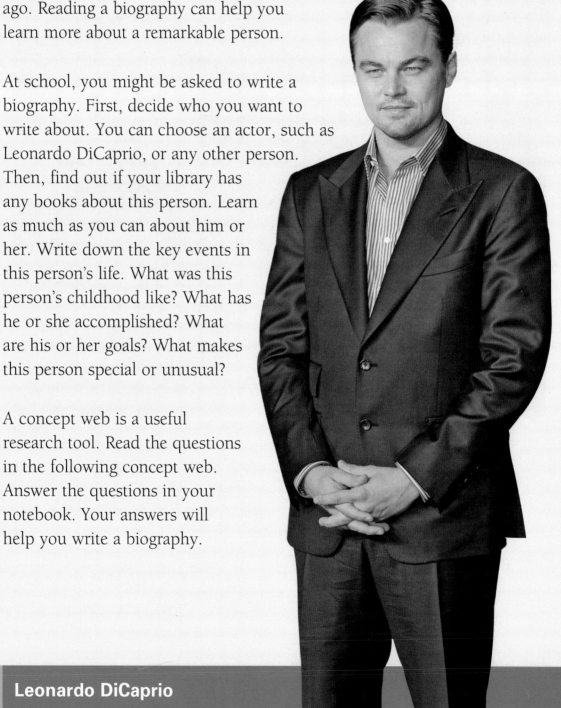

A person's life story can be the subject of a book. This kind of book is called a biography. Biographies describe the lives of remarkable people, such as those who have achieved great success or have done important things to help others. These people may be alive today, or they may have lived many years ago. Reading a biography can help you learn more about a remarkable person.

At school, you might be asked to write a biography. First, decide who you want to write about. You can choose an actor, such as Leonardo DiCaprio, or any other person. Then, find out if your library has any books about this person. Learn as much as you can about him or her. Write down the key events in this person's life. What was this person's childhood like? What has he or she accomplished? What are his or her goals? What makes this person special or unusual?

A concept web is a useful research tool. Read the questions in the following concept web. Answer the questions in your notebook. Your answers will help you write a biography.

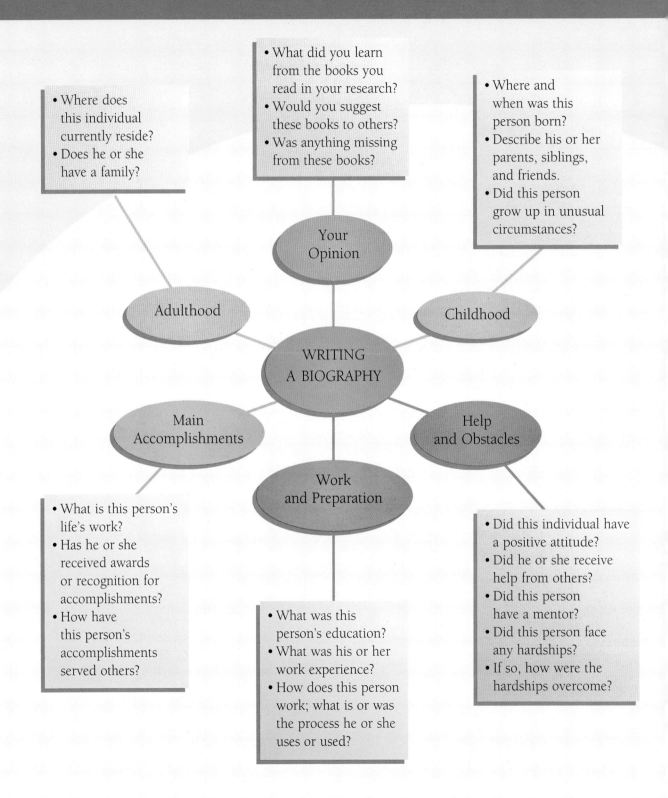

- Where does this individual currently reside?
- Does he or she have a family?

- What did you learn from the books you read in your research?
- Would you suggest these books to others?
- Was anything missing from these books?

- Where and when was this person born?
- Describe his or her parents, siblings, and friends.
- Did this person grow up in unusual circumstances?

Your Opinion

Adulthood

Childhood

WRITING
A BIOGRAPHY

Main
Accomplishments

Help
and Obstacles

Work
and Preparation

- What is this person's life's work?
- Has he or she received awards or recognition for accomplishments?
- How have this person's accomplishments served others?

- What was this person's education?
- What was his or her work experience?
- How does this person work; what is or was the process he or she uses or used?

- Did this individual have a positive attitude?
- Did he or she receive help from others?
- Did this person have a mentor?
- Did this person face any hardships?
- If so, how were the hardships overcome?

Timeline

YEAR	LEONARDO DICAPRIO	WORLD EVENTS
1974	Leonardo DiCaprio is born in Los Angeles on November 11.	*The Sting* wins the Academy Award for Best Picture.
1991	Leonardo is cast as Luke Brower on a television sitcom called *Growing Pains*.	The original *Dallas* television show goes off the air.
1996	*William Shakespeare's Romeo + Juliet* is released, with Leonardo as the male lead.	Nicolas Cage wins the Golden Globe for Best Actor—Drama, for his work in *Leaving Las Vegas*.
1997	*Titanic* is released and becomes the top earning movie to date.	*The Lion King* opens on Broadway.
1998	The Leonardo DiCaprio Foundation is established.	*Titanic* wins the Academy Award for Best Picture.
2005	Leonardo wins a Golden Globe for his work in *The Aviator*.	*The Aviator* wins the Golden Globe for Best Picture—Drama.
2013	Leonardo announces that he is taking a break from acting.	Daniel Day-Lewis wins the Academy Award for Best Actor for his role in *Lincoln*.

Key Words

Academy Awards: awards presented by the Academy of Motion Picture Arts and Sciences for achievements in motion picture production and performance

agent: a person who finds performers for the entertainment industry and helps performers find jobs that suit their skills

audition: a performance staged to try to get a job in the entertainment industry

blockbusters: movies that have financial success

cast: selected as an actor for a show

creativity: the use of the imagination and original ideas

endangered animals: animals that are at risk of no longer living on Earth

environmental activist: a person who takes action to protect the environment

Golden Globe: an award presented by the Hollywood Foreign Press Association recognizing excellence in film and television

imitating: copying someone's behavior

lead: an actor who plays the principal role in a motion picture

movie directors: people who manage the actors and crew making a film

nomination: a list of people who will be considered for an award

relief: aid in times of danger

renewable energy: energy that comes from natural resources and can be used indefinitely

roles: parts played by an actor or singer

scripts: the written text of plays, screenplays, or broadcasts

sitcom: situation comedy that features characters sharing a common environment

Index

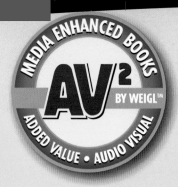

Log on to www.av2books.com

AV² by Weigl brings you media enhanced books that support active learning. Go to www.av2books.com, and enter the special code found on page 2 of this book. You will gain access to enriched and enhanced content that supplements and complements this book. Content includes video, audio, weblinks, quizzes, a slide show, and activities.

AV² Online Navigation

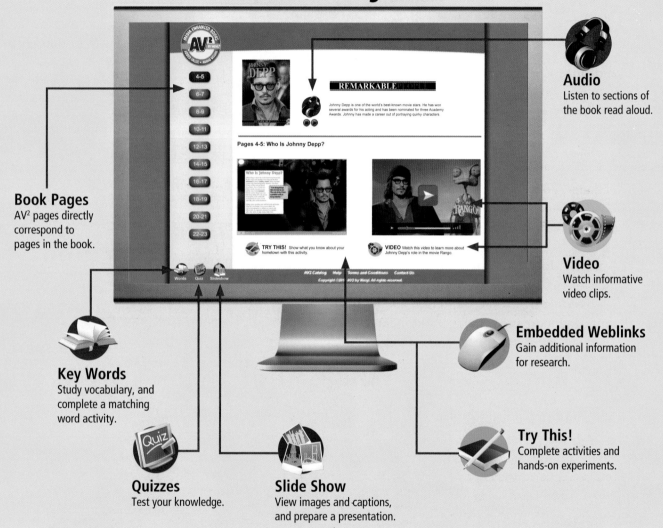

Audio
Listen to sections of the book read aloud.

Book Pages
AV² pages directly correspond to pages in the book.

Video
Watch informative video clips.

Key Words
Study vocabulary, and complete a matching word activity.

Embedded Weblinks
Gain additional information for research.

Quizzes
Test your knowledge.

Slide Show
View images and captions, and prepare a presentation.

Try This!
Complete activities and hands-on experiments.

AV² was built to bridge the gap between print and digital. We encourage you to tell us what you like and what you want to see in the future.

Sign up to be an AV² Ambassador at www.av2books.com/ambassador.